CITIES of the WORLD
ACTIVITY BOOK

GEMMA BARDER
AND
JENNY WREN

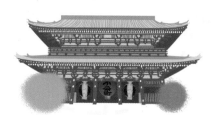

ARCTURUS

CONTENTS

ARCTURUS

This edition published in 2021 by Arcturus Publishing Limited
26/27 Bickels Yard, 151–153 Bermondsey Street,
London SE1 3HA

Author: Gemma Barder
Illustrator: Jenny Wren
Editor: Violet Peto
Designer: Jeni Child
Design Manager: Jessica Holliland
Managing Editor: Joe Harris

ISBN: 978-1-83940-621-8
CH007762NT
Supplier 42, Date 0321, Print run 10676

Printed in Singapore

Vancouver

Seattle

Toronto   Niagara Falls

Chicago

New York

Washington DC

Los Angeles

Miami

Mexico City

Bogotá

Lima

São Paulo

Rio de Janeiro

Santiago

Buenos Aires

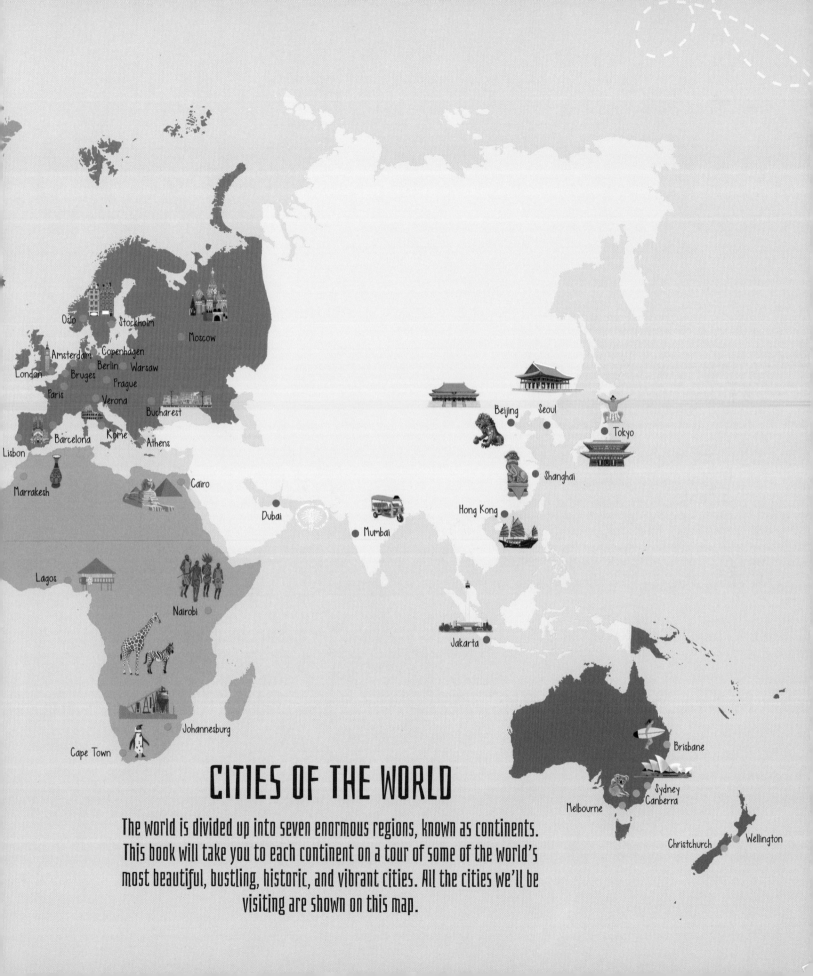

CITIES OF THE WORLD

The world is divided up into seven enormous regions, known as continents. This book will take you to each continent on a tour of some of the world's most beautiful, bustling, historic, and vibrant cities. All the cities we'll be visiting are shown on this map.

NORTH AMERICA

Vancouver
Seattle
Toronto
Niagara Falls
Chicago
New York
Washington
Los Angeles
Miami
Mexico City

The continent of North America is home to 23 countries and some of the most spectacular cities in the world. Your North American adventure starts in the coninent's largest country, Canada, at an attraction that is visited by over 30 million people each year.

NIAGARA FALLS, CANADA

The city of Niagara Falls is named for three waterfalls, over which thunder 568,000 l (150,000 gal) of water per second. Can you find each of the items described below in the big picture?

Write down the coordinates of the square you think they are in.

1. A bird with a twig in its mouth

_____ _____

2. A man carrying a baby

_____ _____

3. A coffee cup

_____ _____

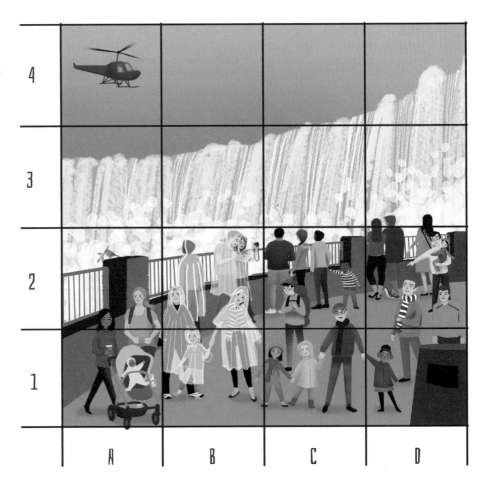

- The three waterfalls that make up Niagara are called the American Falls, the Bridal Veil Falls, and the Horseshoe Falls.

- It is illegal (and quite possibly deadly) to go over the falls in any way.

TORONTO: CN TOWER

Toronto is known for its range of glittering skyscrapers, including the giant CN Tower. The tower is the tallest free-standing structure in the Western Hemisphere and is over 553 m (1,815 ft) tall.

Make this skyline come to life using your pens or pencils. Make it a daytime scene with light glinting off the windows and water, or turn it into night with a starlit sky and shining moon.

▪ Toronto is home to Canada's largest zoo.

▪ It can get pretty chilly in Toronto. The lowest-ever temperature recorded was -33 °C (-27 °F).

VANCOUVER, CANADA

Vancouver is known as a destination for all kinds of winter sports. Its mixture of powder-like snow and not-too-cold weather makes it the perfect place to hit the slopes!

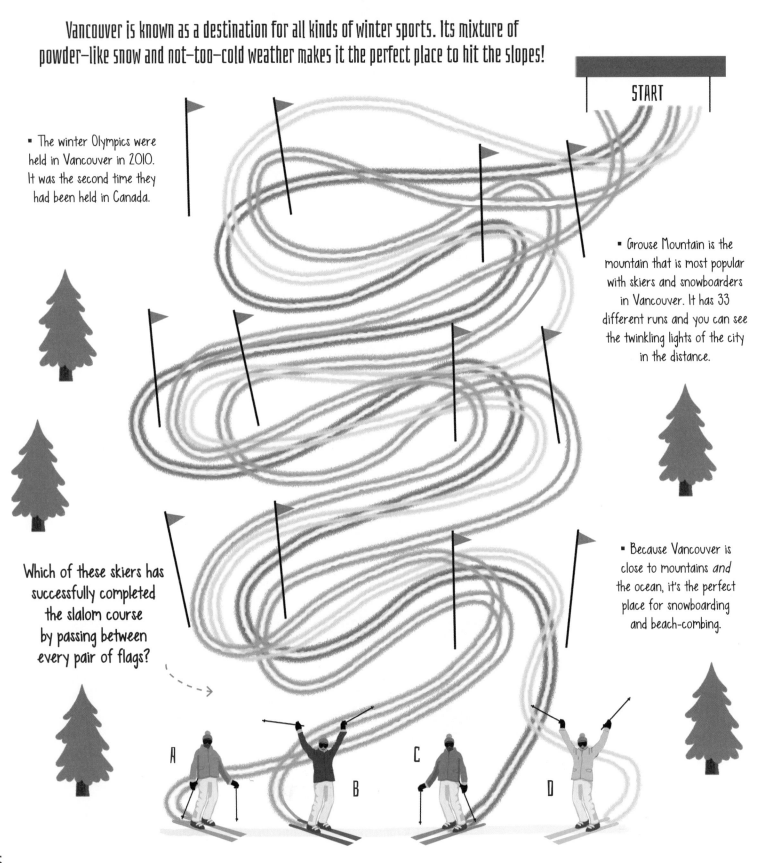

START

- The winter Olympics were held in Vancouver in 2010. It was the second time they had been held in Canada.

- Grouse Mountain is the mountain that is most popular with skiers and snowboarders in Vancouver. It has 33 different runs and you can see the twinkling lights of the city in the distance.

Which of these skiers has successfully completed the slalom course by passing between every pair of flags?

- Because Vancouver is close to mountains and the ocean, it's the perfect place for snowboarding and beach-combing.

A

B

C

D

VANCOUVER: GASTOWN

Gastown was the original settlement for the people who went on to found Vancouver. The area gets its name from "gassy" Jack Deighton, a famous past resident who enjoyed telling long stories in a loud voice!

Finish this picture of Gastown by filling in the missing jigsaw pieces. Can you spot the statue of Gassy Jack?

A   B   C   D   E

NEW YORK, USA

New York City (NYC) is one of the world's most famous cities. Tourists love to visit its museums, art galleries, stores, and Broadway musicals. It's also home to more than eight million people!

Which taxi can make its way through the maze, stopping off at each sight along the way, A, B, or C?

1. Central Park
Central Park has more than 26,000 trees, lots of prehistoric boulders, and 9,000 benches. It's also featured in more than 250 movies!

4. The Empire State Building
After a year and 45 days of building, the Empire State Building was once the tallest skyscraper in the world.

5. The Statue of Liberty
Given to the USA by France, this iconic statue was originally a bright golden-red. It turned green after being outside for over 140 years!

FINISH

6. The American Museum of Natural History
With more than 33 million historical objects behind its doors, you could spend a lot of time in this famous museum.

1. Central Park 2. The Chrysler Building 3. The Flat Iron Building
4. The Empire State Building, 5. The Statue of Liberty, 6. The American Museum of Natural History

Connect the dots in order, and reveal one of NYC's most famous foods.

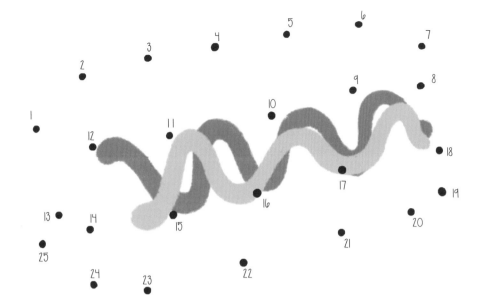

Use pens or pencils to finish the picture (and make it look extra delicious!).

Popular toppings include tomato sauce, mustard, and sauerkraut.

Times Square is a busy place filled with neon lights and vibrant billboards. Can you find the six differences between these pictures?

▪ Hundreds of people gather in Times Square each December 31st for a spectacular New Year celebration.

SEATTLE, USA

Seattle is a city of firsts: the first coffee shop chain,
and the first gas station both originated here.

Which coffee should come next in each order? Look closely and figure out the sequence.

A

B

C

SEATTLE: THE SPACE NEEDLE

The Space Needle was created as part of a future-themed World's Fair. It was based on a sketch of a UFO and has an observation deck at the very top.

To find out the year in which the Space Needle was built, cross out each number that appears more than once in the grid below. Read the remaining numbers from left to right, top to bottom to reveal the answer.

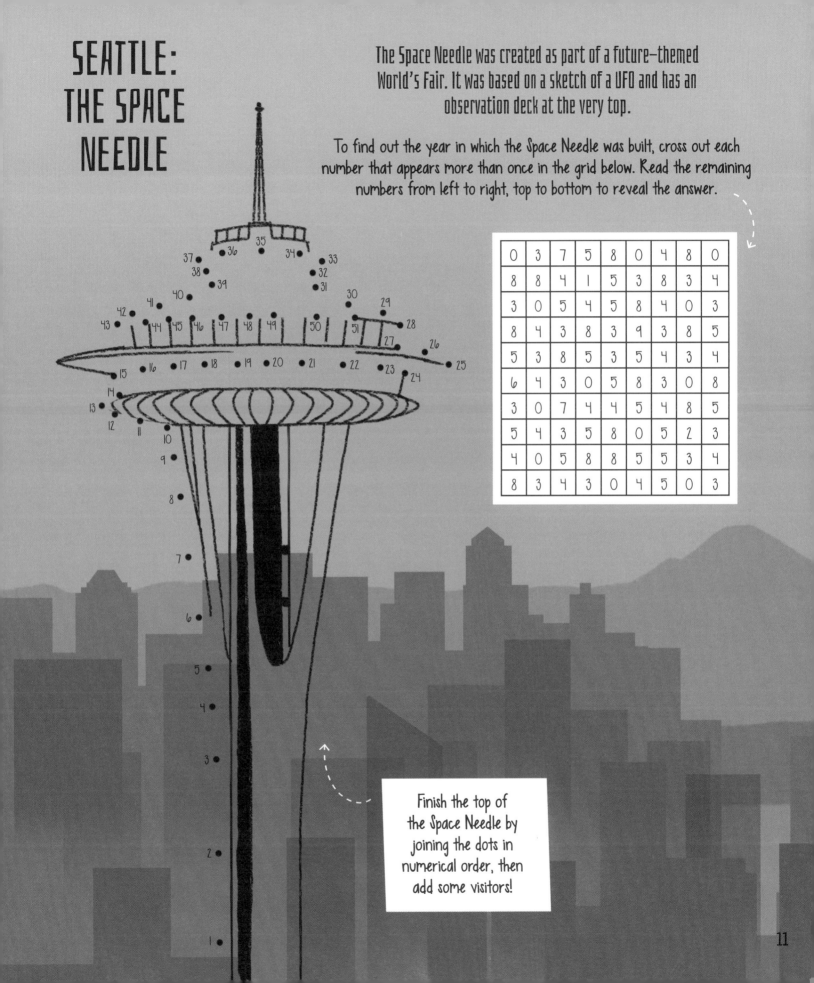

0	3	7	5	8	0	4	8	0
8	8	4	1	5	3	8	3	4
3	0	5	4	5	8	4	0	3
8	4	3	8	3	9	3	8	5
5	3	8	5	3	5	4	3	4
6	4	3	0	5	8	3	0	8
3	0	7	4	4	5	4	8	5
5	4	3	5	8	0	5	2	3
4	0	5	8	8	5	5	3	4
8	3	4	3	0	4	5	0	3

Finish the top of the Space Needle by joining the dots in numerical order, then add some visitors!

WASHINGTON DC, USA

The White House in Washington has been the home of The President of the United States of American since 1800. It has 132 rooms and 35 bathrooms!

Take a look at the pictures below. How many of each can you find in the big picture?

 _____

 _____

 _____

 _____

CHICAGO, USA

Bustling with busy people and full of character, Chicago is one of the USA's most famous cities. Known for its big buildings, and ... Chicago deep-pan pizza!

Work out which pizza belongs to this customer by reading the order:

A stuffed crust pizza with black olives, green bell peppers, pineapple chunks, and no meat.

A

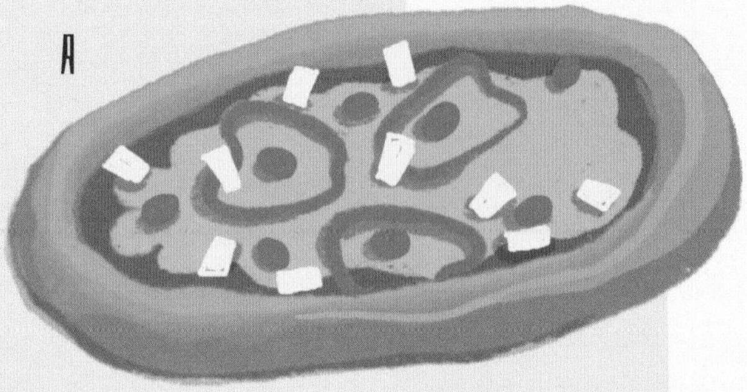

B

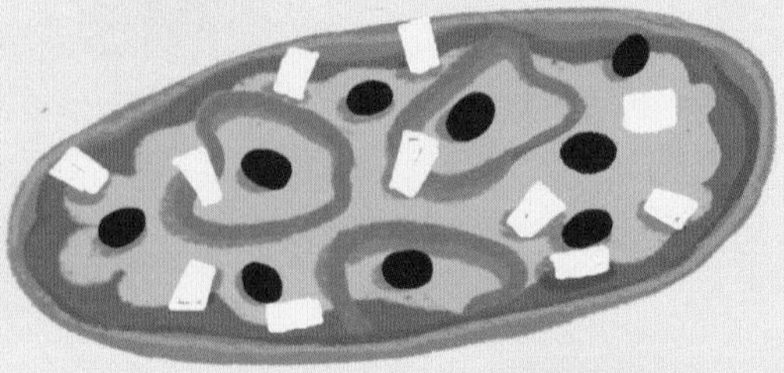

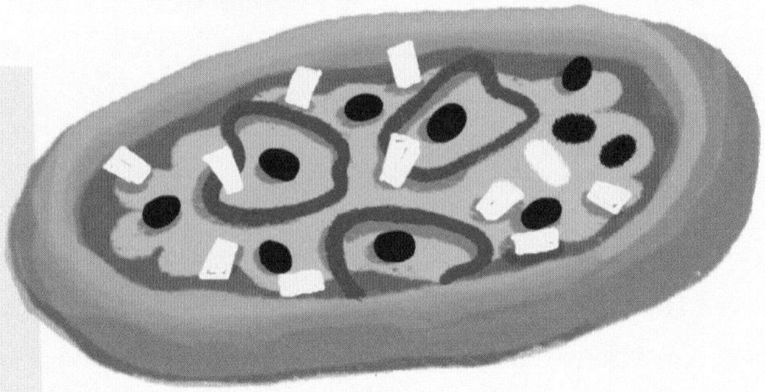

C

D

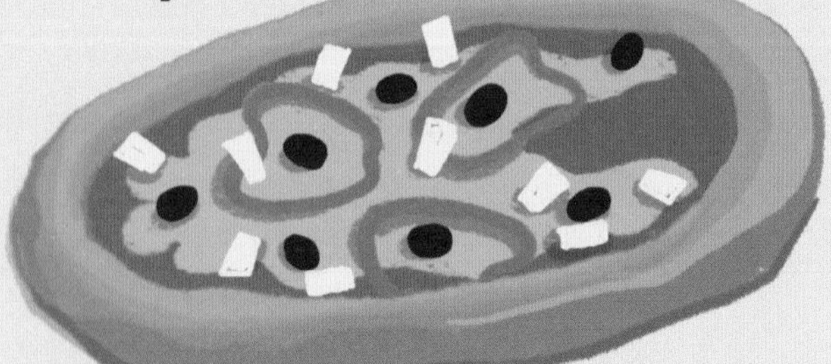

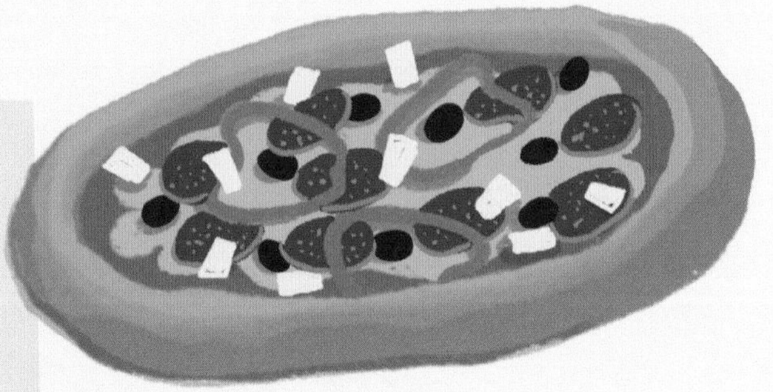

E

MIAMI, USA

Miami isn't only palm trees, beautiful beaches, and rollerblades. It's also home to the world's largest collection of Art Deco architecture and is the only major city in the USA to be founded by a woman.

Miami's South Beach is lined with bright, buildings designed in the Art Deco style. Take a look and see if you can spot the six differences between these two pictures.

If you plan to take a walk along any of Miami's famous beaches, you'll want to look your best while protecting your eyes. Using your pens and pencils, design a pair of fabulous sunglasses to wear!

15

LOS ANGELES, USA

LA is famous for being the home of movies, as well as movie stars! All the big movie companies have studios in LA, which makes it the perfect place to film the next blockbuster!

Take a look at the items below. How many of each can you find on the movie set?

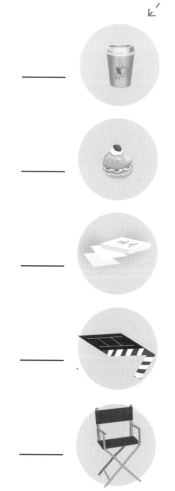

_____

_____

_____

_____

_____

MEXICO CITY, MEXICO

Mexico City, in Central America, is full of life, street food, and people! Although the city is bursting with buildings, crowds, and cars, it also has one of the biggest city parks in the world. The Bosque de Chapultepec park is known as the "lungs" of Mexico City.

Can you guide this tourist through the Bosque de Chapultepec park?

START

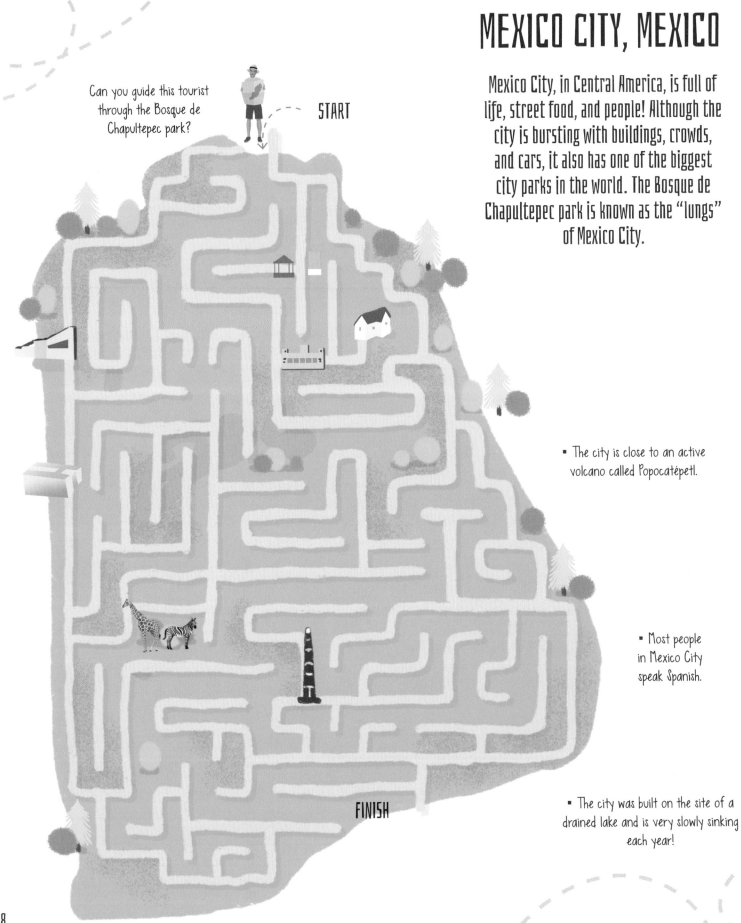

- The city is close to an active volcano called Popocatépetl.

- Most people in Mexico City speak Spanish.

- The city was built on the site of a drained lake and is very slowly sinking each year!

FINISH

On most streets in Mexico City you'll be able to find a street vendor selling delicious food. Can you find all of the dishes shown below in the wordsearch?

TAMALES

BURRITOS

TACOS

ESQUITES

TLACOYOS

ESCAMOLES

H	T	B	U	R	R	I	T	O	S
O	L	S	O	C	A	T	Q	J	E
Y	A	Q	E	J	L	B	E	S	S
F	C	W	A	H	E	M	C	E	N
S	O	Q	M	G	O	A	T	R	J
L	Y	U	J	X	M	I	U	N	I
X	O	R	T	O	U	D	R	Z	V
C	S	Z	L	Q	S	J	F	D	M
H	J	E	S	E	L	A	M	A	T
F	S	E	Q	C	K	L	F	R	K

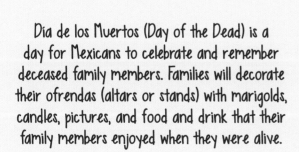

Dia de los Muertos (Day of the Dead) is a day for Mexicans to celebrate and remember deceased family members. Families will decorate their ofrendas (altars or stands) with marigolds, candles, pictures, and food and drink that their family members enjoyed when they were alive.

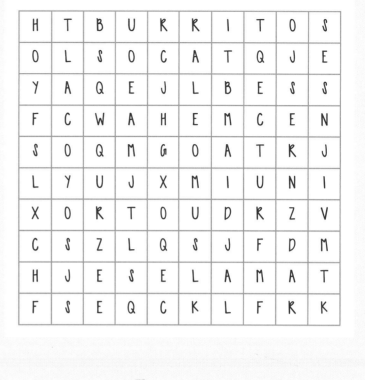

Grab your pencils to finish off this classic Dia de los Muertos mask.

SOUTH AMERICA

South America is made up of 12 countries and includes one of the world's biggest countries, Brazil. This continent is also really important to the environment as it is home to around 40% of the world's plants and animals. South America has deep Spanish and Portuguese influences, which are shown through the food, music, and culture of its countries.

RIO DE JANEIRO, BRAZIL

The city of Rio de Janeiro is dominated by the huge Sugarloaf Mountain. Each day, cable cars take passengers up and down the mountain to see Rio from above.

Which two cable cars are painted exactly the same?

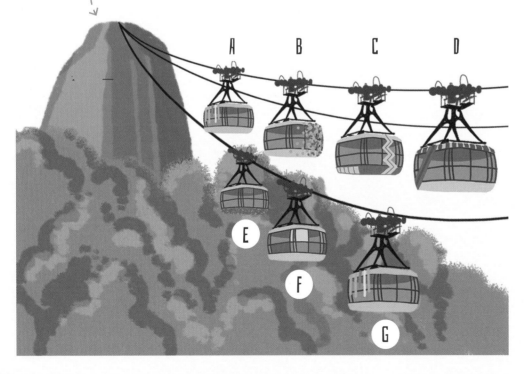

Sugarloaf Mountain is 396 m (1299 ft) tall. Take a look at these famous buildings. Are any of these bigger than Sugarloaf Mountain in real life?

1. Burj Khalifa, Dubai, UAE

2. Empire State Building, New York City, USA

3. Eiffel Tower, Paris, France

RIO DE JANEIRO: CHRIST THE REDEEMER

Discover some interesting facts about Rio's most iconic landmark. Can you guess which are true and which are false?

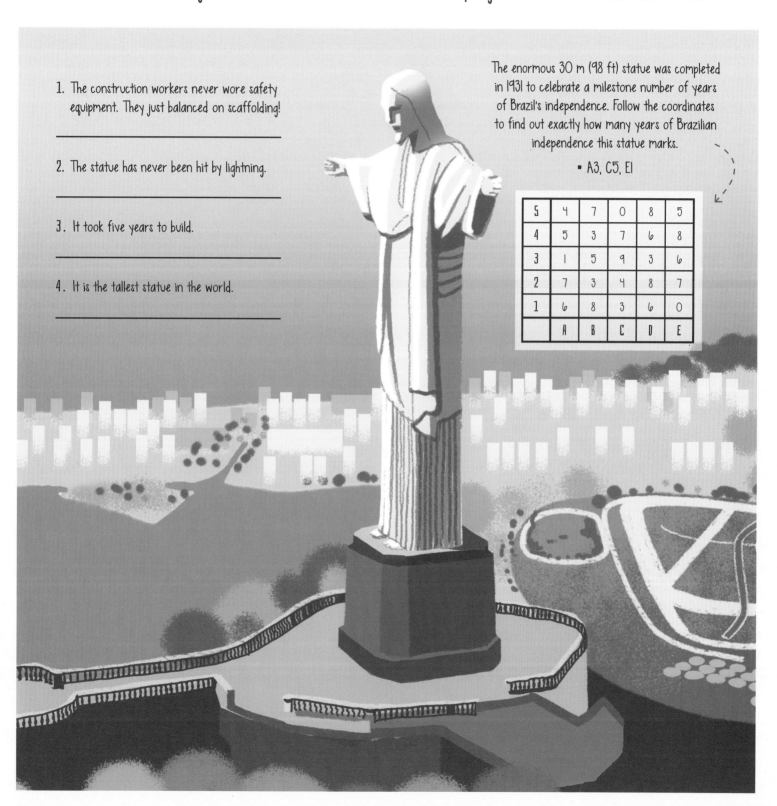

1. The construction workers never wore safety equipment. They just balanced on scaffolding!

_____

2. The statue has never been hit by lightning.

_____

3. It took five years to build.

_____

4. It is the tallest statue in the world.

_____

The enormous 30 m (98 ft) statue was completed in 1931 to celebrate a milestone number of years of Brazil's independence. Follow the coordinates to find out exactly how many years of Brazilian independence this statue marks.

▪ A3, C5, E1

5	4	7	0	8	5
4	5	3	7	6	8
3	1	5	9	3	6
2	7	3	4	8	7
1	6	8	3	6	0
	A	B	C	D	E

SÃO PAULO, BRAZIL

São Paulo is the most-populated city in South America. This is because lots of people come to São Paulo to work in one of the many businesses that are based there. It's also home to lots of people from different nations. It has the largest Italian community in South America, and the most Japanese residents outside of Asia.

Despite being a busy, welcoming place, São Paulo has a reputation for wet weather!

Which umbrella should come next in each sequence?

Some of these unlucky people in Parque do Ibirapuera don't have umbrellas. Can you draw some for them? Give them bright, bold patterns.

SÃO PAULO: BIG BUSINESS

Lots of goods are produced in São Paulo, including many items from the food, textile, design, and technology industries.

Can you place all of these items once in each column, row, and mini grid?

BUENOS AIRES, ARGENTINA

From the famous street art scenes, to the Latin dance clubs, right through to the local passion for soccer, the capital of Argentina is a vibrant hub that is full of life!

Complete this street art scene.

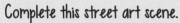

Most of the street artists in Buenos Aires sign their work using a unique "tag" like the ones shown here. Design yours below!

The tango first became popular in Buenos Aires over 100 years ago. Its popularity spread across the globe, but its heart will always be in Argentina. Buenos Aires holds many tango competitions and festivals each year to pay respect to its most famous dance.

Take a look at this couple dancing the tango. Which silhouette is their exact match?

Some say that soccer is the true religion of Argentina. Buenos Aires has the most soccer teams of any city on the planet—a whopping 24!

Which of these soccer players is going to score the goal?

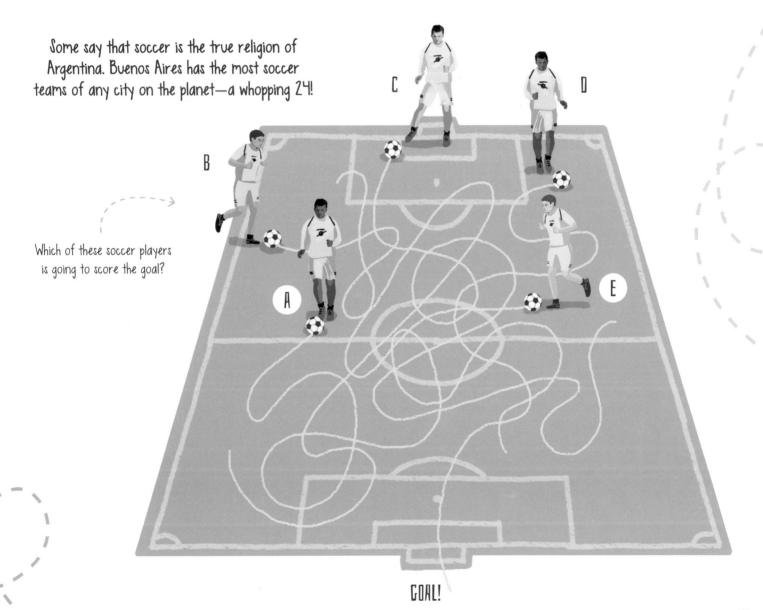

GOAL!

SANTIAGO, CHILE

Santiago is the beautiful capital of Chile. It is surrounded by mountains, including the famous Andes mountain range. Despite being crammed with historical buildings, it also has one of the largest city parks in the world, and lies close to the foot of a dormant volcano.

One of Santiago's biggest attractions is The Mercado Central de Santiago. Visitors go to gaze at the building as much as the stalls and merchandise on offer!

Take a look at the pictures below. Can you find each one in the market scene?

LIMA, PERU

The capital city of Peru is home to more than eight million people. It has stunning beaches, historical buildings (including the Americas' oldest university), and so much to see and do.

Lima's Magic Water Circuit in the Parque de la Reserva is said to be the most spectacular water show in the world. The show mixes light and water and is choreographed to music. Use the guide to help you complete this picture of Lima's Magic Water Fountain show.

LIMA: HUACA PUCLLANA

Huaca Pucllana is a great clay pyramid in central Lima. It was built around 500 CE as a ceremonial and administrative building.

Unscramble the letters to reveal three types of offerings that were left on the Huaca Pucllana stones.

T O Y P E R T

R U F I T

S F H I

BOGOTÁ, COLOMBIA

Fresh fruit, coffee, and bustling streets are just a few of the reasons why Bogotá in Colombia is such a popular place for tourists, as well as for people who live and work there.

FINISH

- 60% of the world's emeralds come from Colombia. The majority of these are sold in Bogotá's Emerald District.

Lots of visitors escape the busy streets and climb Monseratte Mountain. Help these tourists find their way to the top, so they can take in the view from Monserrate Sanctuary.

START

- As the capital city of one of the world's leading coffee-producing countries, Bogotá is home to a thriving coffee scene. Its many coffee shops offer the ultimate coffee-tasting experience.

BOGOTÁ: PLAZA BOLÍVAR

Take a look at this picture of one of Bogotá's most famous squares. Which jigsaw pieces go where?

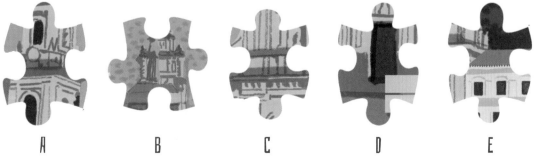

A   B   C   D   E

EUROPE

Oslo
Stockholm
Moscow
Amsterdam
London
Copenhagen
Bruges
Berlin
Warsaw
Prague
Paris
Verona
Bucharest
Barcelona
Lisbon
Rome
Athens

Europe is made up of 44 countries. This continent is nearly 10 million km² (4 million m²) in size, and is home to royalty, some of the most visited countries in the world, and it even has its own rain forests!

LONDON, UK

London is home to nine million people, with millions more visiting each year to see historic sites such as Buckingham Palace, the Tower of London, and St. Paul's Cathedral.

Busy Londoners get around the city using buses, boats, taxis, and a network of underground trains. Can you work out where each of these people want to go?

1

2

3

4

KNIGHTSBRIDGE A

WESTMINSTER B

EARL'S COURT C

MARYLEBONE D

LONDON: THE LONDON EYE

The London Eye was opened for visitors in 2000 and was only meant to be up for five years. However, the giant cantilevered observation wheel was so popular that it has stayed put! In fact, it is now the UK's most popular paid-for attraction.

The 32 capsules on the London Eye represent London's 32 boroughs. However, the cabins are numbered 1—33. Which number is missing?

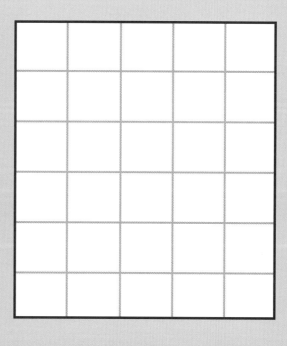

The Crown Jewels are a set of precious items that belong to the monarch of the UK. They include a sceptre, an orb, and the crown itself. They are kept under guard at the Tower of London.

Copy the image, square by square, to draw the royal crown.

BUCHAREST, ROMANIA

The word "Bucharest" can be translated into "beautiful city" and it is easy to see why. Its rows of pretty streets have earned Bucharest the nickname "Little Paris."

Bucharest's Palace of Parliament is the second-largest administrative building in the world, second only to the Pentagon in the USA. It is a very impressive building, but can you guess whether these statements are true or false?

1. It has 10 floors underground.

_____

2. It has 100 rooms.

_____

3. It is the heaviest building in the world

_____

4. It is visible from the Moon.

_____

LISBON, PORTUGAL

Lisbon is the capital of Portugal and is the oldest city in Western Europe.
The earliest part of São Jorge Castle was built in the 5th century.

- The city has over 200 registered football clubs.

- The oldest and the smallest bookshops in the world can be found in Lisbon.

- The Vasco da Gama bridge is the second-longest bridge in Europe. It is 17 km (11 mi) long.

Take a close look at this scene of São Jorge Castle. How many of each picture can you count?

 _____   _____   _____

PARIS, FRANCE

Paris is a city famous for fashion, food, and art. Visitors can browse the shops, sit at an outdoor café and enjoy a pastry, or even visit the famous Louvre art gallery to look at the Mona Lisa.

One of Paris' most well-known landmarks is the Eiffel Tower. Take a look at these two images and see if you can spot the six differences between them.

- During cold weather, the tower shrinks by about 15 cm (6 in).

- It is 324 m (1,063 ft) tall.

- There are 1,665 steps to the top of the tower (but most people take the elevator!).

ROME, ITALY

As the capital of Italy, Rome is an important and busy place for lots of Italians. It is also one of the most ancient cities in the world.

The famous Colosseum in Rome was completed in 80 CE, so it is just under 2,000 years old! Take a look at the silhouettes and see which one matches the Colosseum perfectly.

A

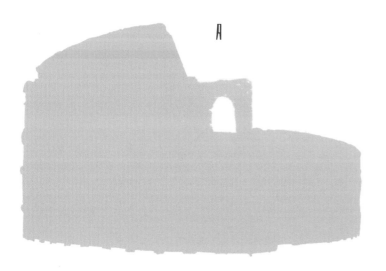

B

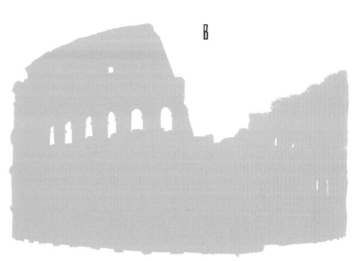

C

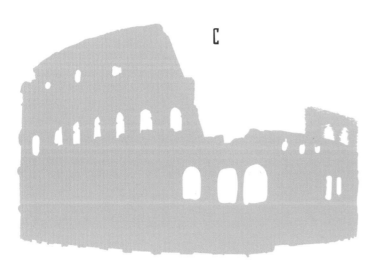

D

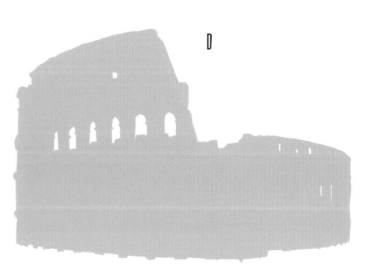

VERONA, ITALY

The city of Verona is famous for being the city where William Shakespeare set his play, *Romeo and Juliet*.

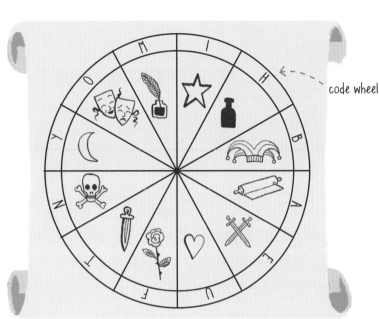

code wheel

Juliet's balcony

Each year, hundreds of people leave messages under Juliet's balcony in Verona.
Use the code wheel to reveal a secret message below.

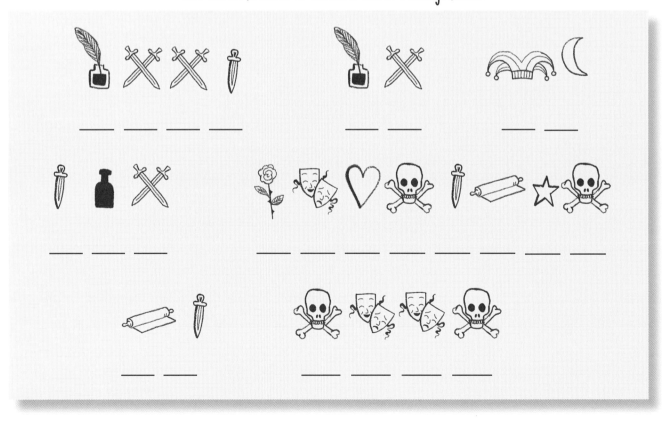

STOCKHOLM, SWEDEN

Stockholm is a beautiful city, above ground and underneath! Its subway is sometimes called the world's longest art gallery, as it is full of paintings and sculptures.

Gamla Stan is the name of Stockholm's old town. It is a great example of a medieval town, with narrow streets, and beautiful buildings.

Take a look at this row of buildings. Can you unscramble the letters on the signs to figure out what kind of stores they are?

A — CFAÉ

B — GORRCEY

C — BTECUHR

D — BKAREY

A _____ B _____ C _____ D _____

- The city is made up of 14 islands connected by more than 50 bridges.

- At Easter, children dress up as witches, in old clothes. They then go from house to house exchanging drawings for treats.

- During the second half of June, it doesn't get very dark in Stockholm. Locals have a celebration each year to celebrate midsummer, called Midsommardagen.

BRUGES, BELGIUM

The capital of Belgium is famous for its historical buildings, waffles, and of course, chocolate! Each year the city square is transformed into a magical Christmas market with thousands of people visiting from all over the world.

Take a look at this box of chocolates. Match each of the chocolates into pairs to find the odd one out.

- There is a whole museum in Bruges dedicated to chocolate.

- More than 100 swans call Bruges home, and can be seen gracefully gliding down the city's many canals.

- There are around 50 castles in and around the city.

OSLO, NORWAY

Despite being the capital of Norway, Oslo is mainly made up of forest. The city contains many beautiful buildings and has a set of islands off its coast.

Edvard Munch's "The Scream" is one of the world's most famous paintings and was donated to the National Gallery of Oslo in 1910.

See if you can create your own painting depicting an emotion, using the style of Edvard Munch.

- Each year, Oslo gives London a Christmas tree to display in Trafalgar Square.

- The people of Oslo are the healthiest in Norway!

- The city used to be called Christiania.

COPENHAGEN, DENMARK

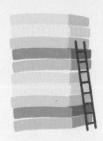

Copenhagen has been named as one of the happiest cities in the world.
The people who live in Copenhagen, and those who go to visit, can see why. Clean air,
narrow, winding streets, and bicycles everywhere. What could be better?

Famous Danish writer Hans Christian Andersen wrote more than 150
fairy tales and is recognized in Copenhagen
with a statue of one of his best-known characters.

Can you spot the five differences between these
two pictures of The Little Mermaid statue?

1. A royal ruler thinks he's wearing a fancy new outfit, but he's actually wearing nothing at all!

2. The princess can feel something small and lumpy in her bed, despite all the mattresses she is lying on!

3. This little bird can't quack and doesn't think he is very pretty ... until he grows up!

Use the clues to name three other famous stories
written by Hans Christian Andersen.

AMSTERDAM, THE NETHERLANDS

There are 165 canals in Amsterdam, and more bridges than in Venice! This beautiful and unique city is also famous for its tulips, cycle-loving residents, and the impressive Rijksmuseum.

Can you figure out which bunch of tulips is the odd one out?

A   B   C   D

Oh dear, this bike won't be wheeling along the canal paths any time soon! Can you find all six of the missing pieces and put it back together?

PRAGUE, CZECH REPUBLIC

This city has many beautiful and ancient buildings. The Vltava river flows through the middle of the city.
The most famous bridge to cross the river is called the Charles Bridge.

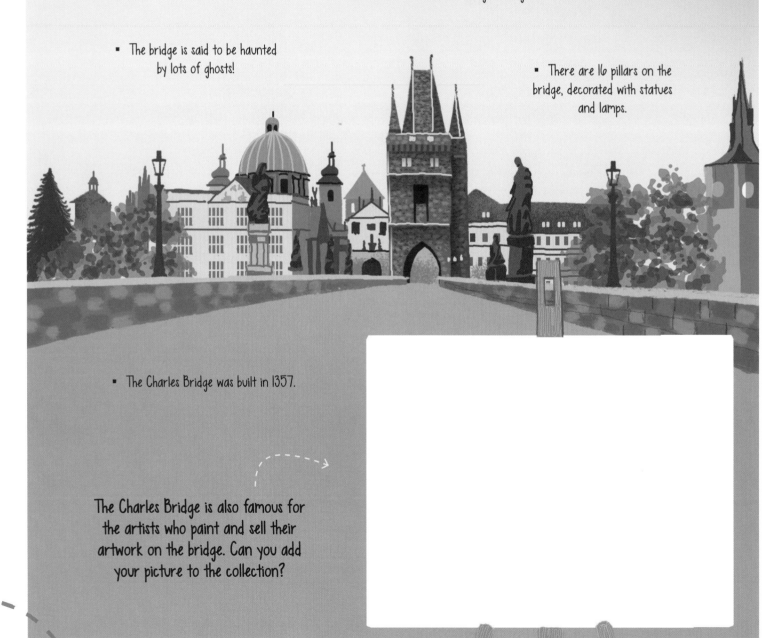

- One legend says that builders mixed raw eggs into the mortar to make the bridge stronger!

- The bridge is said to be haunted by lots of ghosts!

- There are 16 pillars on the bridge, decorated with statues and lamps.

- The Charles Bridge was built in 1357.

The Charles Bridge is also famous for the artists who paint and sell their artwork on the bridge. Can you add your picture to the collection?

Prague has many wonderful sights to see. One of the best places to view them all is at the top of a tall tower that sits on a hill overlooking the city.

P	W	H	Y	U
Y	O	U	O	E
S	T	H	W	Y
O	A	S	A	O
W	H	U	R	L
L	S	Y	A	L
A	I	W	U	S
H	S	H	N	Y

Cross out all the letters that appear more than once in the grid to discover the name of this famous tower.

_ _ _ _ _ _

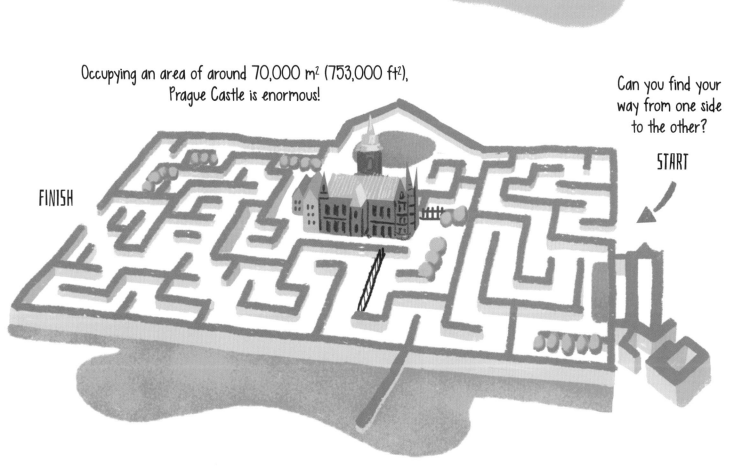

Occupying an area of around 70,000 m² (753,000 ft²), Prague Castle is enormous!

Can you find your way from one side to the other?

START

FINISH

BERLIN, GERMANY

Berlin is the capital of Germany, and it is also the country's biggest city, with 3.7 million people calling it home.

The Brandenburg Gate is a huge structure through which people used to enter and leave Berlin. On top is a sculpture of a Quadriga (chariot) driven by Victoria, the Goddess of Victory.

Can you spot which silhouette is the perfect match to the Quadriga? Learn more fun facts about Berlin as you go!

A

B

• Berlin's city symbol is a black bear which features on the Berlin flag.

C

• Did you know that this city has three opera houses and around 170 museums?

D

• Berlin has the longest open-air gallery in the world!

BARCELONA, SPAIN

Barcelona is the capital of Catalonia, an area of Spain. It is famous for its delicious tapas food and inspiring architecture, including houses and a church designed by Antoni Gaudí.

La Sagrada Familia is a church that was started in 1882 ... and is still being built! Architects and engineers are still working on Gaudi's magnificent creation and believe it could be finished in 2026.

Take a look at this image and see if you can complete the picture before the builders in real life!

C

D

A

E

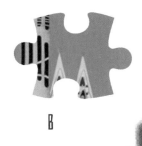
B

▪ Flamenco is a traditional Spanish art form which combines music and dance. These passionate performances can be seen all over Barcelona.

▪ There were no beaches in the city of Barcelona until 1992 when it hosted the Olympic Games. The council created several beaches for the celebration.

▪ The museum for the soccer team FC Barcelona is the most-visited museum in the city.

ATHENS, GREECE

Records show that Greece's capital could be over 3,000 years old, which means that Athens is packed with history.

The skyline of Athens is dominated by The Parthenon, a temple dedicated to the goddess Athena. Thousands of tourists visit the Parthenon each year. Take a look at this tourist's photos to see which two images are the same.

- Athens has more stages than the West End in London and Broadway in New York put together!

- Athens was the first place in the world to decide on something by voting. It is known as the birthplace of democracy.

- Europe's highest ever temperature was recorded in Athens. A scorching 48 °C (118.4 °F)!

MOSCOW, RUSSIA

With 11.9 million people living there, the capital of Russia is a very busy city! Luckily, it also has one of the world's largest metro systems to transport all its inhabitants.

Although Moscow is known for the historic buildings inside the walls of the Kremlin, it's also filled with modern skyscrapers and expensive apartment buildings.

St. Basil's Cathedral in Red Square is one of the most iconic sites on the planet, but how much can you remember? Take a good look at this picture for two minutes, then turn the page to see if you can answer the questions.

It can get very cold in Moscow. The lowest temperature ever recorded was -42 °C (-44 °F)!

Use the guide below to create a picture of street musicians keeping warm in traditional Russian clothing

What can you remember?

1. How many birds were in the sky?

_____

2. Was the dog spotted or striped?

_____

3. Was the sun out?

_____

4. What vehicle was at the bottom of the scene?

_____

5. Did the sign say "open" or "closed"?

_____

WARSAW, POLAND

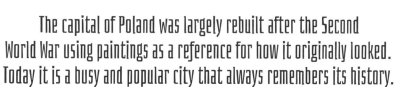

The capital of Poland was largely rebuilt after the Second
World War using paintings as a reference for how it originally looked.
Today it is a busy and popular city that always remembers its history.

Warsaw is famous for its donuts, called paczki, which can be found all over the city.
Can you work out which bakery is selling the cheapest donut?

Paczki   **PACZKI**   **PACZKI**

A

$$12 + 8 - 4 =$$
_____

B

$$3 + 3 + 3 =$$
_____

C

$$5 \times 3 - 2 =$$
_____

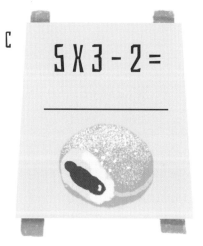

- The world's narrowest house is in Poland. It is only 4.9 ft (152 cm) wide!

- Warsaw is known as "Phoenix City" because it has been rebuilt so many times.

- It is one of the world's smaller capital cities, with 1.8 million people living there.

Marrakesh · Cairo · Lagos · Nairobi · Cape Town · Johannesburg

AFRICA

Africa is the second-largest continent on the planet and is made up of 54 countries. It is home to diverse and ancient cultures, as well as spectacular scenery and majestic animals. We're starting our African adventure in the city of Marrakesh, in Morocco.

MARRAKESH, MOROCCO

The busy marketplaces in Marrakesh are called "souks." They sell many different goods and are often crowded with residents, as well as tourists in search of a bargain! Can you find these items in the souk?

- Many of the goods sold at the souk are handcrafted by locals.

- Vendors sell a variety of vibrant spices in the souk. These are used a lot in North African cooking.

CAPE TOWN, SOUTH AFRICA

Cape Town is known for being a cultural hub as well as for having magnificent mountains and beautiful beaches. Sitting above all of this is Table Mountain, which is covered in beautiful wildflowers from August to September.

Can you find your way up the mountain by following this sequence of flowers in order? You can move up, down, left, and right, but not diagonally.

1
2
3

- 1,470 different types of flower grow on the mountainside.

FINISH

- At least two couples get engaged at the top of Table Mountain every month.

- The cable car that takes people up and down Table Mountain is nearly 100 years old! It began operating in 1929.

START

CAPE TOWN: BOULDERS BEACH

It might be hard to imagine, but penguins live in Africa, too! These African penguins made their home on Boulders Beach in 1982 and have lived there ever since. The species is close to extinction, so they are officially protected by the Cape Nature Conservation.

Can you find the matching pair? Only two of these penguins are identical.

JOHANNESBURG, SOUTH AFRICA

Johannesburg is the largest city in South Africa.
It became popular in 1886 when gold was
discovered, and has been growing ever since.

Which path in this gold mine will lead you to the nuggets of gold?

- Johannesburg is home
  to the world's largest
  man-made forest.

START

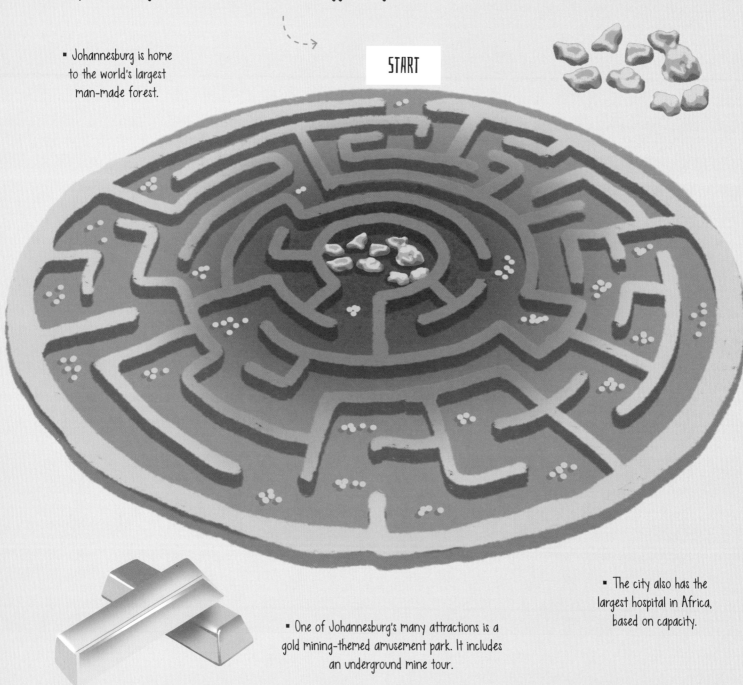

- One of Johannesburg's many attractions is a
  gold mining-themed amusement park. It includes
  an underground mine tour.

- The city also has the
  largest hospital in Africa,
  based on capacity.

LAGOS, NIGERIA

Lagos is sometimes called the New York of Nigeria thanks to its busy nature, but it also has stunning white sandy beaches (which you definitely won't find in New York!).

Can you spot two things in this beach bag that won't be needed for a day at the beach?

Read the clues to find out which beach hut is being described.

- The hut has a light straw roof.
- The hut has a yellow door.
- The hut's number is higher than 10.

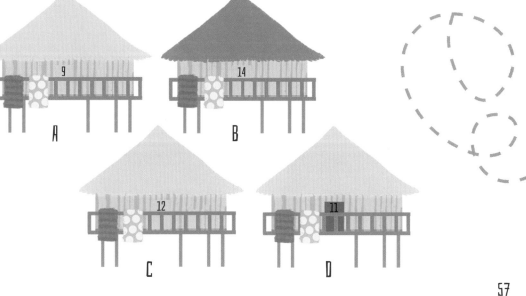

A 9

B 14

C 12

D 11

NAIROBI, KENYA

Nairobi is a buzzing city complete with bustling markets, galleries, and skyscrapers, with amazing animals only a few miles away.

One of Nairobi's many attractions is Nairobi National Park, where visitors can go on safari. Travel in your safari truck through the maze, visiting each animal along the way.

START

You won't have to travel far from Nairobi to meet a giraffe. Which of these is taller, which is shorter, and which is the same height as a giraffe?

1. African elephant

2. Double-decker bus

3. T. rex

FINISH

NAIROBI: THE BOMAS OF KENYA

Nairobi city is home to Bomas of Kenya, a tourist village which holds performances showcasing Kenya's rich and diverse cultural heritage.

Can you spot eight differences between these two pictures of Kenyan dancers?

- Nairobi has the highest number of shopping malls in the whole of Kenya!

- The city of Nairobi was built on the site of a swamp.

- National Independence Day is celebrated on December 12th.

CAIRO, EGYPT

Cairo is Egypt's capital and is the largest city in the country. It is situated along the bank of the river Nile, and is famous for the Great Pyramids and Sphinx.

Take a look at this image of the Great Pyramids and Sphinx on a scorching day in Egypt. Which silhouette matches perfectly?

A

B

C

D

- The Sphinx stands guard by the pyramids. It has the body of a lion and the head of a pharaoh.

- The pyramids were built as tombs for the rulers of Ancient Egypt, who were called pharaohs.

- The Sphinx is more than 4,500 years old

CAIRO: THE NILE

The Nile is the world's longest river. It is also a popular tourist destination, with riverboat cruises taking passengers to see all the famous historical sites.

- The Nile flows into the Mediterranean Sea.
- The Nile is 4,132 m (6,650 km) long.
- It is at least 30 million years old!

Take a look at this picture of a riverboat cruiser. Can you work out which of the circles fit into the big picture?

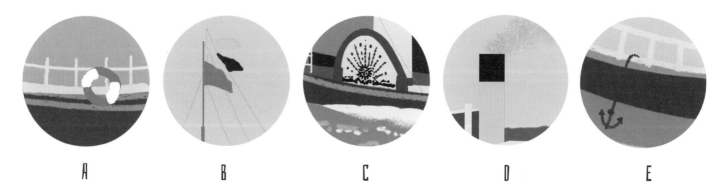

A   B   C   D   E

ASIA

Beijing • Seoul
• Tokyo
• Shanghai
Hong Kong
Dubai • Mumbai

Jakarta

Asia is the biggest and most-populated continent. It is home to 48 countries, the Himalayas, the Gobi Desert, and some of the busiest cities in the world.

We're starting in Japan ...

TOKYO, JAPAN

Tokyo is the capital of Japan and is the largest urban area in the world. Its mix of ancient tradition with modern living makes it a unique city.

Sushi is a Japanese dish made with rice and seafood or vegetables.

Tokyo has a long history, which can be seen through its many temples. The most famous of these is the Sensō-ji temple which has more than 30 million visitors each year.

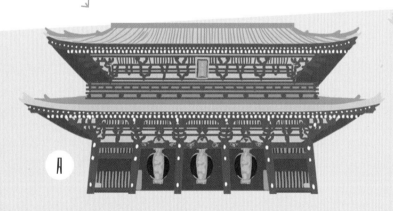

A

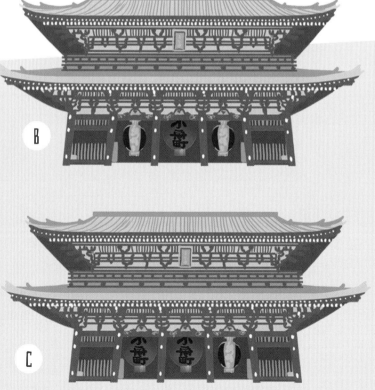

B

C

Can you see which two images of the Sensō-ji temple are exactly the same?

It is so busy in Tokyo that the Shibuya Crossing is not only essential, it has become a bit of a landmark. 2,500 people can cross the Shibuya Crossing at one time!

Look at the picture of the Shibuya Crossing and answer these questions by writing down the correct grid references.

1. Is the yellow umbrella in E2 or B3?

2. In which grid reference is the heart-shaped balloon?

3. How many trees are there in G3?

4. In which grid reference is the sign with a star on it?

5. Start in A5, move 2 squares right, and 4 squares down. What do you see in the square?

■ The temple was founded in 645 CE in dedication to the Buddhist goddess of mercy, Kannon.

HONG KONG, CHINA

Hong Kong is full of skyscrapers, fine food, and fun. Home to more than seven million people, it is also one of the most densely-populated cities in the world!

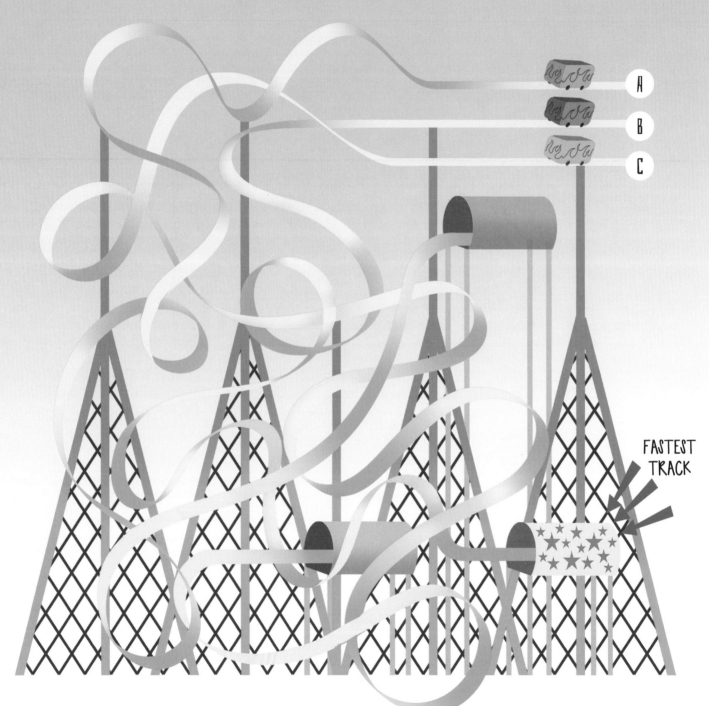

Hong Kong has lots of theme parks for all those people to have fun in. Follow the lines to see which roller coaster car will finish the ride first.

HONG KONG: VICTORIA BAY

At Victoria Bay you can see where old meets new. Traditional fishing boats called "junk boats" float along with towering skyscrapers in the background.

See if you can copy this picture of a junk boat.

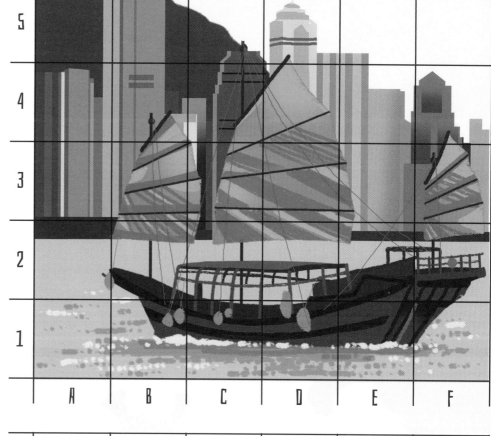

• There are more than 250 islands that make up Hong Kong.

• Many apartment buildings here don't have a fourth floor as the number is considered to be unlucky.

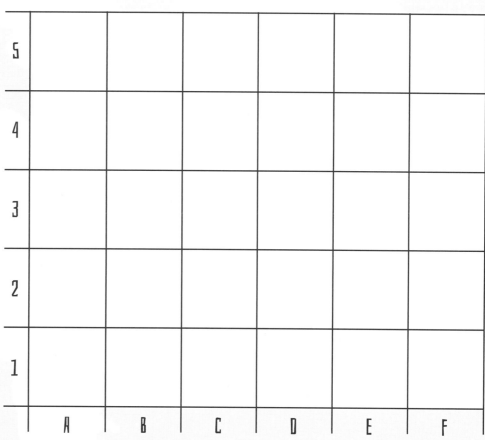

- The name Shanghai means "upon the sea."

- The city started as a small fishing village.

- It is well-liked by shoppers as it has everything from sprawling markets to luxury shopping malls.

SHANGHAI, CHINA

Shanghai is the most-populated city in China. It has a population of more than 24 million people, one of the longest underground railway systems in the world, and an impressive set of skyscrapers. However, it is also a beautiful city, and home to ancient parks such at the Yuyuan Garden.

Look closely at the big picture of Yuyuan Garden and see if you can spot all of the details shown below.

BEIJING, CHINA

One of the most famous sights in Beijing has to be The Great Wall of China. Read some interesting facts below, then see if you can make your way along the wall!

- It is the longest man-made structure in the world.

- The Great Wall was built to protect China from invaders.

- It is 21,196.18 km (13,170.70 mi) in length.

Make your way along the wall completing the number pyramid on each tower as you go. Each number is the sum of the two numbers directly beneath it. Write the final number in each flag.

BEIJING: THE FORBIDDEN CITY

The Forbidden City was once home to the Emperor of China. Today it houses the Palace Museum and is one of the most-visited places in China.

Chinese guardian lions are ornamental statues which were placed at the Forbidden City to protect it from harmful spirits, as well as people! Can you find this lion's perfect silhouette?

A

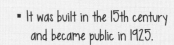

B

- There are 980 buildings and more than 8,700 rooms inside the Forbidden City.

- It was built in the 15th century and became public in 1925.

C

- It was named "Forbidden" because not everyone was allowed inside the walls. Only high-ranking families were invited.

D

MUMBAI, INDIA

Mumbai is the biggest and richest city in the whole of India. It is a busy city with packed trains and congested traffic. Away from the central buzz, there are a variety of ancient and interesting sights to see.

The Elephanta caves are a set of cave temples dedicated to the Hindu god, Shiva.

Can you fit these missing jigsaw pieces into the main picture of the cave temples?

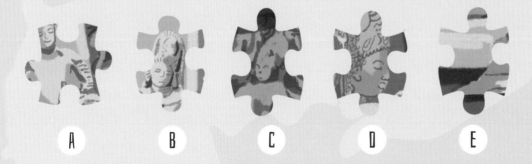

Getting around Mumbai can be tricky. Lots of people choose to dive into a tuk-tuk, a small vehicle that can dart in and out of traffic.

Finish off this image of a tuk-tuk. Make it as bright as possible!

Can you help these people get to their waiting tuk-tuks?

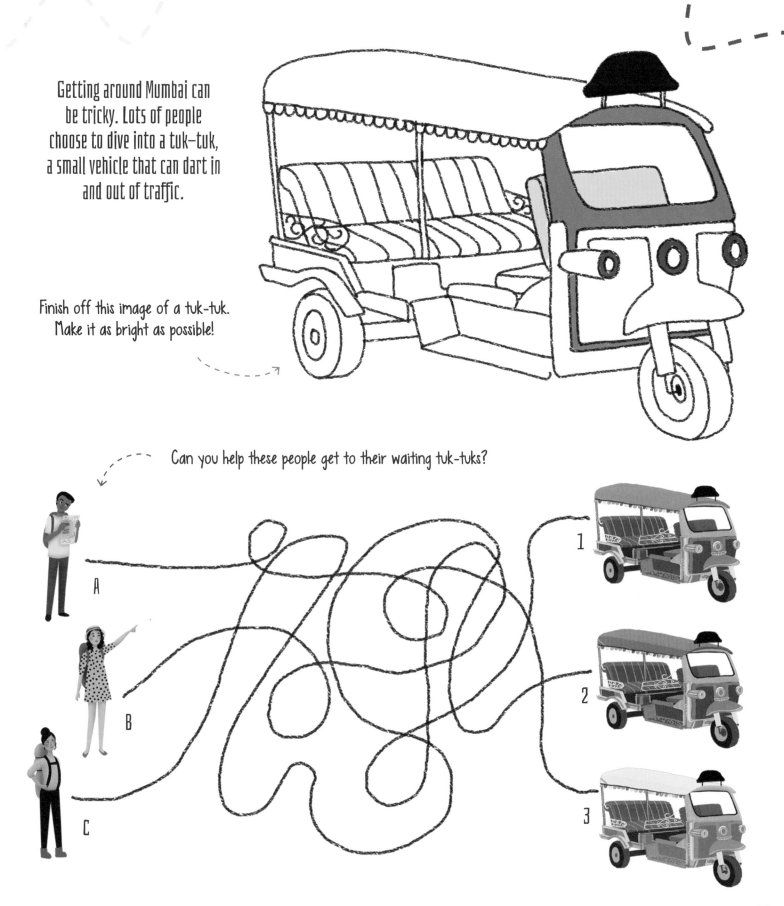

A

B

C

1

2

3

DUBAI, UAE

Dubai is a young city in the United Arab Emirates, but it is growing all the time. Just over 40 years ago it only had one high-rise building—it now has hundreds!

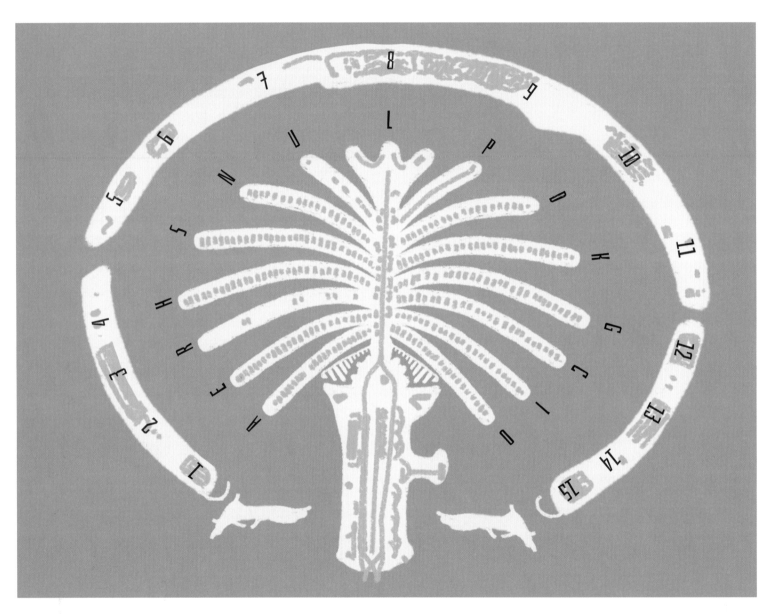

The Palm Islands in Dubai are one of the most eye-catching parts of the city. The construction of these man-made islands began in 2001. Look at this aerial view of the islands and use the code to find out what materials they are made from.

5.1.6.10   1.6.10   3.15.13.11

_ _ _ _   _ _ _   _ _ _ _

JAKARTA, INDONESIA

Although it is one of the cheapest cities to live in, the capital of Indonesia can also be very crowded, especially on the roads where there are more cars than people!

The National Monument in Jakarta is one of the city's most visited spots. It is 132 m (433 ft) tall and stands as a symbol of Indonesia's independence.

Take a look at these two pictures and see if you can spot the six differences between them.

- It is rude to pat someone on the head in Indonesia, as that is where their spirit is believed to live.

- Because of its many rivers and rising sea levels, Jakarta is prone to flooding. It is one of the world's fastest-sinking cities.

- Experts believe that most of the city could be submerged by 2050. As a result, the government is considering moving the country's capital to another city.

SEOUL, SOUTH KOREA

The mixture of cutting-edge fashion and culture, combined with its long and complicated history, makes Seoul a unique city.

If you take a walk by the N Seoul Tower you will notice a sea of padlocks, locked at the base of the tower. Couples come to the tower to declare and seal their love forever with traditional padlocks, or locks made out of wood, photographs, or even paper!

Take a look at these padlocks. Can you match them into pairs?

SEOUL: GYEONGBOKGUNG PALACE

The Gyeongbokgung Palace was completed in 1395, but it has been the site of many battles over hundreds of years. It is now home to a museum, and restoration work continues to this day.

FINISH

Springtime is beautiful in Seoul, as this is when the cherry blossom trees come into bloom. Find your way through this maze of blossom to get to the palace.

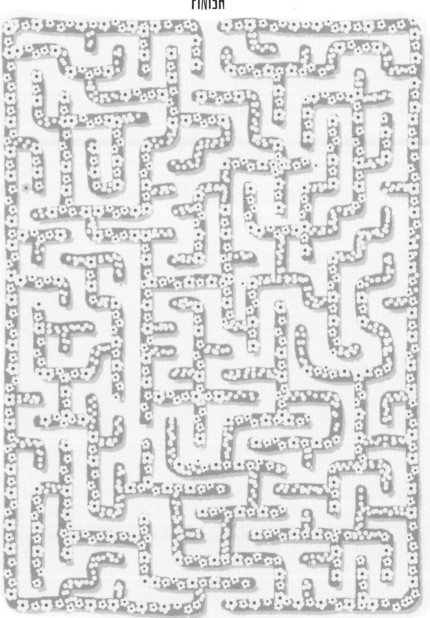

START

OCEANIA

The continent of Oceania includes Australia, New Zealand, and all the islands of Melanesia, Micronesia, and Polynesia. From small islands to one of the biggest countries in the world, Oceania packs a lot in!

CANBERRA, AUSTRALIA

Canberra is the capital of Australia and is full of important buildings and museums. It is built around Lake Burley Griffin, an impressive man-made lake.

Each March, Canberra hosts a magnificent balloon festival with hundreds of hot-air balloons taking to the sky.

Give this balloon a design all of your own!

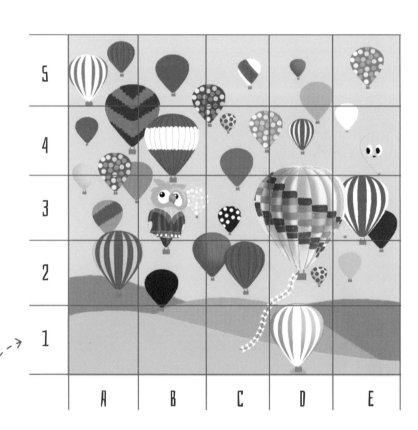

Answer these questions by giving the correct coordinates.

1 Where are the two matching striped balloons? _____

2 Where is the balloon that hasn't taken off? _____

3 Where is the plain red balloon? _____

4 Where is the balloon shaped like an owl? _____

CANBERRA: THE NATIONAL ZOO AND AQUARIUM

The National Zoo and Aquarium is one of Canberra's most popular destinations.
With many different species to discover, it is one of the best zoos in the country.

The zoo houses animals native to Australia, as well as introduced species. Can you tell which three of these animals are NOT native to Australia?

- Canberra is just over 100 years old (making it quite a young city).

- The city has been called the "bush capital" because of its many nature reserves.

- Canberra also has a NASA base!

capybara

dingo

platypus

echidna

panda

Tasmanian devil

meerkat

emu

kangaroo

wombat

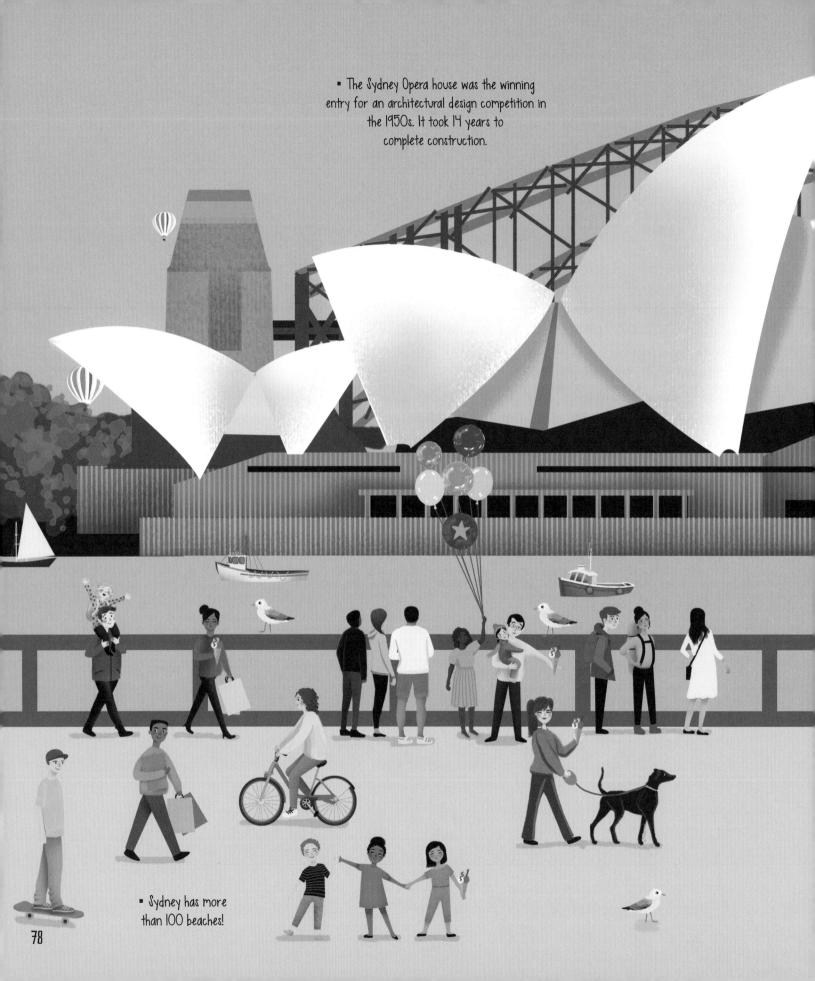

▪ The Sydney Opera house was the winning entry for an architectural design competition in the 1950s. It took 14 years to complete construction.

▪ Sydney has more than 100 beaches!

SYDNEY, AUSTRALIA

The city of Sydney is built around its port, which is home to one of the world's most famous landmarks: the Sydney Opera House.

How many of each of these can you find in the big picture?

_____

_____

_____

_____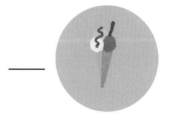

MELBOURNE, AUSTRALIA

Melbourne is often voted one of the best cities to live in. Its mixture of weather, relaxed lifestyle, and lots to do make Melburnians some of the happiest people around!

Australians love cricket. The Melbourne Cricket Ground is one of the world's most famous sporting grounds. Known to most Australians as simply "The G."

S	E	S	M	A	S	E	M	A	F
T	T	I	L	N	D	A	W	M	I
U	A	R	U	C	H	S	I	E	E
M	P	R	T	A	B	T	C	E	L
P	M	B	E	R	R	U	K	S	D
S	B	O	W	L	E	R	E	L	E
L	W	E	R	T	Y	U	T	I	R
L	L	A	B	A	S	D	F	G	H

Can you find all these cricketing words in the wordsearch?

BALL   RUNS

WICKET   BOWLER

BAT   FIELDER

STUMPS

MELBOURNE: FED SQUARE

Federation Square (or "Fed Square" to locals) is a public square, and art, music, and sports venue.

Lots of different performances take place at Fed Square.

Draw a costume onto this person. Will they be a dancer, a singer or something else entirely?

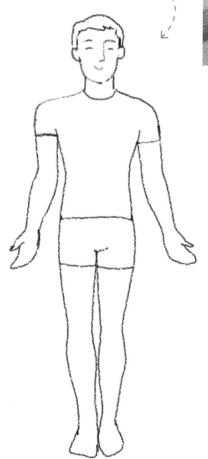

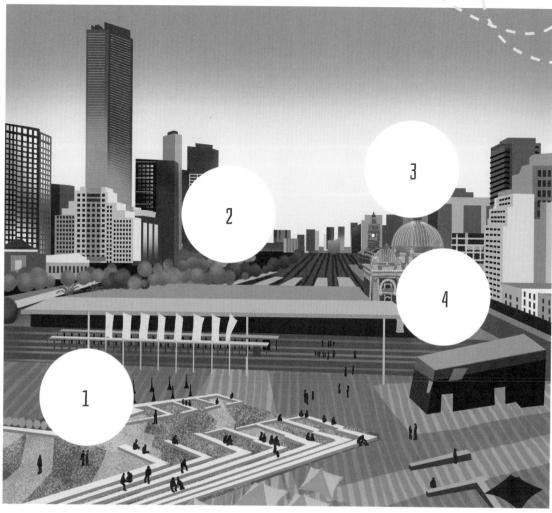

Take a look at this picture of Fed Square. Can you work out which of the circles fit into the big picture?

A

B

C

D

E

F

BRISBANE, AUSTRALIA

Although it is smaller than Melbourne and Sydney, Brisbane is a popular city thanks to its fabulous weather, fashionable locals, and friendly atmosphere.

Brisbane is home to the largest koala sanctuary in Australia. Can you find three matching pairs of cuddly koalas?

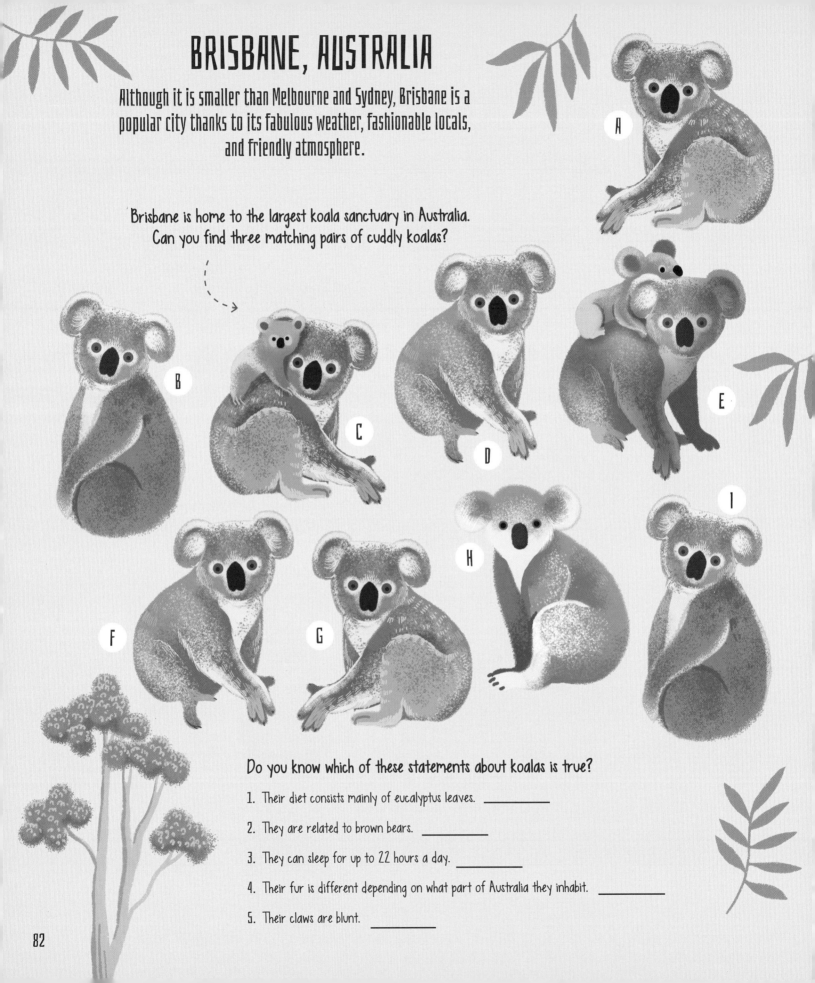

A

B

C

D

E

F

G

H

I

Do you know which of these statements about koalas is true?

1. Their diet consists mainly of eucalyptus leaves. _____

2. They are related to brown bears. _____

3. They can sleep for up to 22 hours a day. _____

4. Their fur is different depending on what part of Australia they inhabit. _____

5. Their claws are blunt. _____

BRISBANE: STORY BRIDGE

Story Bridge is one of Brisbane's most well-known landmarks.
Visitors can even climb to the very top!

Can you spot five differences between these two pictures?

- Brisbane has an underground opera house!

- It has an average of 283 days of sunshine a year.

- Story Bridge is twinned with Jacques Cartier Bridge in Montréal, Canada.

WELLINGTON, NEW ZEALAND

Wellington is the capital of New Zealand and one of the best-loved cities in the country. Residents are known for being super-friendly and the city is very eco-friendly, too!

A

The Wellington Cable Car carries passengers from the bustle of the city to the botanical gardens, taking in great views along the way.

Can you work out which cable car has the most passengers?

B

- The city is known as "Windy Wellington" thanks to strong winds coming through the Cook Straight.

- It's a popular destination for fans of Lord of the Rings, as some of the movie was filmed there.

C

WELLINGTON: ZEALANDIA

Zealandia is an urban ecosanctuary. Its goal is to turn the land back to how it was before humans arrived!

Can you fit each of the four Zealandia plants and animals once in each row, column, and mini grid?

Can you find the zealandia flower that is the odd one out?

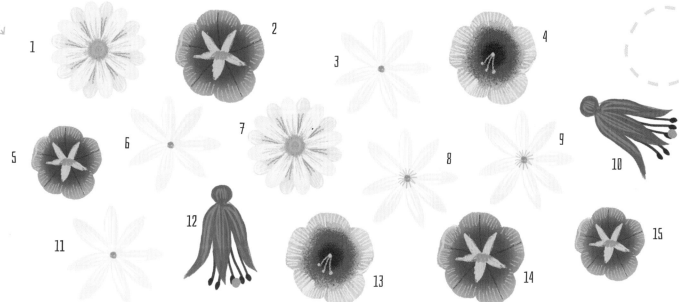

1
2
3
4
5
6
7
8
9
10
11
12
13
14
15

CHRISTCHURCH, NEW ZEALAND

Christchurch is smaller than Wellington, but it is full of quirky sights and fun things to do!

Hagely Park was opened in 1855 and has been Christchurch's largest park ever since. Take a look at this scene and see if you can find the coordinates for each of these circles. Then count the butterflies!

How many butterflies can you see?

1 _____   2 _____   3 _____   _____

QUIZ

We're at the end of our world tour of cities. How much have you learned along the way? See if you can answer the following questions. All the answers can be found on page 98.

1. How many bathrooms does The White House have?

   a) 132

   b) 35

2. What is Chicago known for?

   a) Art Deco architecture

   b) Deep-pan pizza

3. Which city is dominated by Sugarloaf Mountain?

   a) Marrakesh

   b) Rio de Janeiro

4. Which dance first became popular in Buenos Aires?

   a) Tango

   b) Flamenco

5. Which Shakespeare play is set in Verona?

   a) *Macbeth*

   b) *Romeo and Juliet*

6. Which city gives London a Christmas tree each year?

   a) Oslo

   b) Rome

7. Which of these is in Johannesburg?

   a) Africa's largest lake

   b) Africa's largest hospital

8. Where is the Shibuya Crossing?

   a) Melbourne

   b) Tokyo

9. Where is the world's tallest building?

   a) Dubai

   b) Christchurch

10. Which capital city holds a balloon festival each March?

   a) London

   b) Canberra

ANSWERS

PAGE 4:

1. A2

2. D2

3. A1

PAGE 6:

D

PAGE 7:

1. C

2. B

3. D

4. E

5. A

PAGE 8: A

PAGE 9:

One of NYC's most famous foods is the hot dog.

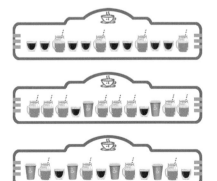

PAGE 10:

PAGE 11:

1962

PAGES 12–13:

2

5

2

5

PAGE 14:

D

PAGE 15:

PAGES 16-17:

9

3

5

3

5

PAGE 18

PAGE 19:

H	T	B	U	R	R	I	T	O	S
O	L	S	O	C	A	T	Q	J	E
Y	A	Q	E	J	L	B	E	S	S
F	C	W	A	H	E	M	C	E	N
S	O	Q	M	G	O	A	T	R	J
L	Y	U	J	X	M	I	U	N	I
X	O	R	T	O	U	D	R	Z	V
C	S	Z	L	Q	S	J	F	D	M
H	J	E	S	E	L	A	M	A	T
F	S	E	Q	C	K	L	F	R	K

PAGE 20:

A and G

1. Burj Khalifa, Dubai, UAE
   Yes: 830 m (2,723 ft)

2. Empire State Building,
   New York City, USA
   Yes: 443 m (1454 ft)

3. Eiffel Tower, Paris, France
   No: 324 metres (1063 ft)

PAGE 21:

1. True.

2. False. It has been hit many times, causing serious damage.

3. True.

4. False. The tallest statue in the world is actually the Statue of Unity in India.

100 years.

PAGE 22:

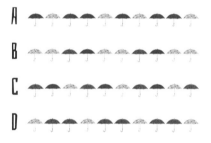

PAGE 23:

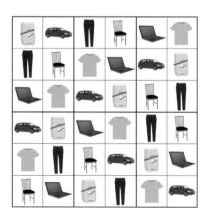

PAGE 25:

3

D

PAGES 26-27:

PAGE 29:

POTTERY

FISH

FRUIT

PAGE 30:

PAGE 31:

1. A

2. C

3. D

4. E

5. B

PAGE 32:

1. D Marylebone

2. B Westminster

3. A Knightsbridge

4. C Earl's Court

PAGE 33:

13 is missing because it is considered an unlucky number.

PAGE 34:

1. False. It has 8 floors underground.

2. False. It has 1100 rooms.

3. True.

4. True.

PAGE 35:

 12   3   4

PAGE 36:

PAGE 37:

D

PAGE 38:

MEET ME BY THE FOUNTAIN AT NOON

PAGE 39:

A. CAFÉ

B. GROCERY

C. BUTCHER

D. BAKERY

PAGE 40:

PAGE 42:

1. The Emperor's New Clothes

2. The Princess & the Pea

3. The Ugly Duckling

PAGE 43:

D

PAGE 45:

Petrin

PAGE 46:

C

PAGE 47:

A. 5

B. 3

C. 4

D. 2

E. 1

PAGE 48:

B and D

PAGE 50:

1. 7

2. Spotted

3. Yes

4. Bicycle

5. Open

PAGE 51:

A. 16

B. 9

C. 13

B is the bakery selling the cheapest donut.

PAGES 52–53:

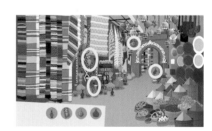

PAGE 54:

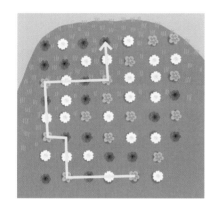

PAGE 55:

PAGE 56:

PAGE 57:

Hot water bottle

Winter hat

Hut C

PAGE 58:

1. Shorter

2. Taller

3. They are the same!

PAGE 59:

PAGE 60:

C

PAGE 61:

1. B

2. D

3. C

PAGES 62-63:

B and E

PAGE 63:

1. B3

2. F5

3. I

4. C4

5. A dog

PAGE 64:

B

PAGES 66–67:

PAGE 68:

PAGE 69:

D

PAGE 70:

1. C

2. B

3. D

4. A

5. E

PAGE 71:

A. 3

B. 1

C. 2

PAGE 72:

SAND AND ROCK

PAGE 73:

PAGE 74:

PAGE 75:

PAGE 76:

1. A5 and C2

2. D1

3. B5

4. B3

PAGE 77:

Meerkat (native to Africa)
Panda (native to China)
Capybara (native to South America)

PAGES 78-79:

4 🎈

5 🕊

3 ⛵

4 🦆

PAGE 80:

S	E	S	M	A	S	E	M	A	F
T	T	I	L	N	D	A	W	M	I
U	A	R	U	C	H	S	I	E	E
M	P	R	T	A	B	T	C	E	L
P	M	B	E	R	R	U	K	S	D
S	B	O	W	L	E	R	E	L	E
L	W	E	R	T	Y	U	T	I	R
L	L	A	B	A	S	D	F	G	H

PAGE 81:

1. C
2. D
3. B
4. E

PAGE 82:

A and G

B and I

D and F

1. True
2. False
3. True
4. True
5. False

PAGE 83:

PAGE 84:

C 11 passengers

PAGE 85:

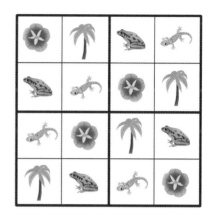

6 ✳

PAGE 86:

1. J2 🐨

2. C2 🐊

3. C5 🏃

5 butterflies

PAGE 88

1. b) 35

2. b) Deep-pan pizza

3. b) Rio de Janeiro

4. a) Tango

5. b) *Romeo and Juliet*

6. a) Oslo

7. b) Africa's largest hospital

8. b) Tokyo

9. a) Dubai

10. b) Canberra